Prayer
Journal

Jennifer R. Laird

Daily Verse

DATE:_____

Bible Verse:

Thoughts & Notes About The Verse

Prayer Requests:

Daily Verse

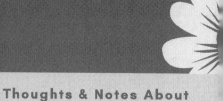

DATE:_____

Bible Verse:

Thoughts & Notes About
The Verse

Prayer Requests:

Daily Verse

DATE:_____

Bible Verse:

Thoughts & Notes About The Verse

Prayer Requests:

Daily Verse

DATE:_____

Bible Verse:

Thoughts & Notes About The Verse

Prayer Requests:

Daily Verse

DATE:_____

Bible Verse:

Thoughts & Notes About The Verse

Prayer Requests:

Daily Verse

DATE:_____

Bible Verse:

**Thoughts & Notes About
The Verse**

Prayer Requests:

WEEKLY VERSE SUMMARY

M

T

W

TH

FRI

SAT

SUN

Church Notes

VERSES MENTIONED DURING CHURCH

☐ _____ ☐ _____

☐ _____ ☐ _____

☐ _____ ☐ _____

☐ _____ ☐ _____

OVERALL MESSAGE FROM SERMON

MY NOTES

PRAYER REQUESTS

My Notes

Daily Verse

DATE:_____

Bible Verse:

Thoughts & Notes About The Verse

Prayer Requests:

Daily Verse

DATE:_____

Bible Verse:

Thoughts & Notes About The Verse

Prayer Requests:

Daily Verse

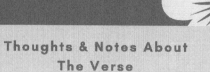

DATE:_____

Bible Verse:

Thoughts & Notes About The Verse

Prayer Requests:

Daily Verse

DATE:_____

Bible Verse:

Thoughts & Notes About The Verse

Prayer Requests:

Daily Verse

DATE:_____

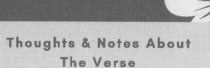

Bible Verse:

Thoughts & Notes About The Verse

Prayer Requests:

Daily Verse

DATE:_____

Bible Verse:

Thoughts & Notes About The Verse

Prayer Requests:

WEEKLY VERSE SUMMARY

M

T

W

TH

FRI

SAT

SUN

Church Notes

VERSES MENTIONED DURING CHURCH

☐ _____ ☐ _____

☐ _____ ☐ _____

☐ _____ ☐ _____

☐ _____ ☐ _____

OVERALL MESSAGE FROM SERMON

MY NOTES

PRAYER REQUESTS

My Notes

Daily Verse

DATE:_____

Bible Verse:

Thoughts & Notes About The Verse

Prayer Requests:

Daily Verse

DATE:_____

Bible Verse:

**Thoughts & Notes About
The Verse**

Prayer Requests:

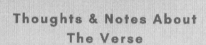

Daily Verse

DATE:_____

Bible Verse:

Thoughts & Notes About The Verse

Prayer Requests:

Daily Verse

DATE:_____

Bible Verse:

Thoughts & Notes About The Verse

Prayer Requests:

Daily Verse

DATE: _____

Bible Verse:

Thoughts & Notes About The Verse

Prayer Requests:

Daily Verse

DATE:_____

Bible Verse:

Thoughts & Notes About The Verse

Prayer Requests:

WEEKLY VERSE SUMMARY

M

T

W

TH

FRI

SAT

SUN

Church Notes

VERSES MENTIONED DURING CHURCH

☐ _____   ☐ _____

☐ _____   ☐ _____

☐ _____   ☐ _____

☐ _____   ☐ _____

OVERALL MESSAGE FROM SERMON

MY NOTES

PRAYER REQUESTS

My Notes

Daily Verse

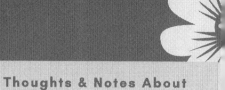

DATE:_____

Bible Verse:

Thoughts & Notes About The Verse

Prayer Requests:

Daily Verse

DATE:_____

Bible Verse:

Thoughts & Notes About The Verse

Prayer Requests:

Daily Verse

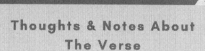

DATE:_____

Bible Verse:

Thoughts & Notes About The Verse

Prayer Requests:

Daily Verse

DATE:_____

Bible Verse:

Thoughts & Notes About The Verse

Prayer Requests:

Daily Verse

DATE:_____

Bible Verse:

**Thoughts & Notes About
The Verse**

Prayer Requests:

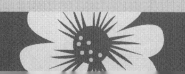

Daily Verse

DATE:_____

Bible Verse:

Thoughts & Notes About The Verse

Prayer Requests:

WEEKLY VERSE SUMMARY

M

T

W

TH

FRI

SAT

SUN

Church Notes

VERSES MENTIONED DURING CHURCH

☐ _____   ☐ _____
☐ _____   ☐ _____
☐ _____   ☐ _____
☐ _____   ☐ _____

OVERALL MESSAGE FROM SERMON

MY NOTES

PRAYER REQUESTS

My Notes

Daily Verse

DATE:_____

Bible Verse:

Thoughts & Notes About The Verse

Prayer Requests:

Daily Verse

DATE:_____

Bible Verse:

Thoughts & Notes About The Verse

Prayer Requests:

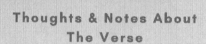

Daily Verse

DATE:_____

Bible Verse:

Thoughts & Notes About The Verse

Prayer Requests:

Daily Verse

DATE:_____

Bible Verse:

Thoughts & Notes About The Verse

Prayer Requests:

Daily Verse

DATE:_____

Bible Verse:

Thoughts & Notes About The Verse

Prayer Requests:

Daily Verse

DATE:_____

Bible Verse:

**Thoughts & Notes About
The Verse**

Prayer Requests:

WEEKLY VERSE SUMMARY

M

T

W

TH

FRI

SAT

SUN

Church Notes

VERSES MENTIONED DURING CHURCH

☐ _____ ☐ _____

☐ _____ ☐ _____

☐ _____ ☐ _____

☐ _____ ☐ _____

OVERALL MESSAGE FROM SERMON

MY NOTES

PRAYER REQUESTS

My Notes

Daily Verse

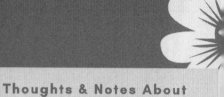

DATE:_____

Bible Verse:

Thoughts & Notes About The Verse

Prayer Requests:

Daily Verse

DATE:_____

Bible Verse:

Thoughts & Notes About The Verse

Prayer Requests:

Daily Verse

DATE:_____

Bible Verse:

Thoughts & Notes About The Verse

Prayer Requests:

Daily Verse

DATE:_____

Bible Verse:

Thoughts & Notes About The Verse

Prayer Requests:

Daily Verse

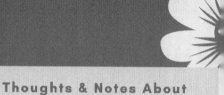

DATE:_____

Bible Verse:

Thoughts & Notes About The Verse

Prayer Requests:

Daily Verse

DATE: _____

Bible Verse:

Thoughts & Notes About The Verse

Prayer Requests:

WEEKLY VERSE SUMMARY

M

T

W

TH

FRI

SAT

SUN

Church Notes

VERSES MENTIONED DURING CHURCH

☐ _____   ☐ _____
☐ _____   ☐ _____
☐ _____   ☐ _____
☐ _____   ☐ _____

OVERALL MESSAGE FROM SERMON

MY NOTES

PRAYER REQUESTS

My Notes

Daily Verse

DATE:_____

Bible Verse:

Thoughts & Notes About The Verse

Prayer Requests:

Daily Verse

DATE:_____

Bible Verse:

Thoughts & Notes About The Verse

Prayer Requests:

Daily Verse

DATE:_____

Bible Verse:

Thoughts & Notes About The Verse

Prayer Requests:

Daily Verse

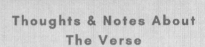

DATE:_____

Bible Verse:

**Thoughts & Notes About
The Verse**

Prayer Requests:

Daily Verse

DATE:_____

Bible Verse:

Thoughts & Notes About The Verse

Prayer Requests:

Daily Verse

DATE:_____

Bible Verse:

Thoughts & Notes About The Verse

Prayer Requests:

WEEKLY VERSE SUMMARY

M

T

W

TH

FRI

SAT

SUN

Church Notes

VERSES MENTIONED DURING CHURCH

- [ ] _____
- [ ] _____
- [ ] _____
- [ ] _____
- [ ] _____
- [ ] _____
- [ ] _____
- [ ] _____

OVERALL MESSAGE FROM SERMON

MY NOTES

PRAYER REQUESTS

My Notes

Daily Verse

DATE:_____

Bible Verse:

Thoughts & Notes About The Verse

Prayer Requests:

Daily Verse

DATE:_____

Bible Verse:

Thoughts & Notes About The Verse

Prayer Requests:

Daily Verse

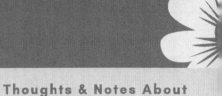

DATE:_____

Bible Verse:

Thoughts & Notes About The Verse

Prayer Requests:

Daily Verse

DATE:_____

Bible Verse:

Thoughts & Notes About
The Verse

Prayer Requests:

Daily Verse

DATE:_____

Bible Verse:

Thoughts & Notes About The Verse

Prayer Requests:

Daily Verse

DATE:_____

Bible Verse:

Thoughts & Notes About The Verse

Prayer Requests:

WEEKLY VERSE
SUMMARY

M

T

W

TH

FRI

SAT

SUN

Church Notes

VERSES MENTIONED DURING CHURCH

☐ _____   ☐ _____

☐ _____   ☐ _____

☐ _____   ☐ _____

☐ _____   ☐ _____

OVERALL MESSAGE FROM SERMON

MY NOTES

PRAYER REQUESTS

My Notes

Daily Verse

DATE:_____

Bible Verse:

Thoughts & Notes About The Verse

Prayer Requests:

Daily Verse

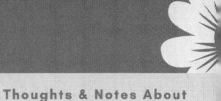

DATE:_____

Bible Verse:

Thoughts & Notes About
The Verse

Prayer Requests:

Daily Verse

DATE:_____

Bible Verse:

Thoughts & Notes About The Verse

Prayer Requests:

Daily Verse

DATE:_____

Bible Verse:

Thoughts & Notes About The Verse

Prayer Requests:

Daily Verse

DATE:_____

Bible Verse:

**Thoughts & Notes About
The Verse**

Prayer Requests:

Daily Verse

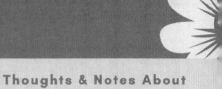

DATE:_____

Bible Verse:

Thoughts & Notes About The Verse

Prayer Requests:

WEEKLY VERSE
SUMMARY

M

T

W

TH

FRI

SAT

SUN

Church Notes

VERSES MENTIONED DURING CHURCH

☐ _____   ☐ _____

☐ _____   ☐ _____

☐ _____   ☐ _____

☐ _____   ☐ _____

OVERALL MESSAGE FROM SERMON

MY NOTES

PRAYER REQUESTS

My Notes

Daily Verse

DATE:_____

Bible Verse:

Thoughts & Notes About The Verse

Prayer Requests:

Daily Verse

DATE:_____

Bible Verse:

Thoughts & Notes About The Verse

Prayer Requests:

Daily Verse

DATE:_____

Bible Verse:

Thoughts & Notes About The Verse

Prayer Requests:

Daily Verse

DATE:_____

Bible Verse:

Thoughts & Notes About The Verse

Prayer Requests:

Daily Verse

DATE:_____

Bible Verse:

Thoughts & Notes About The Verse

Prayer Requests:

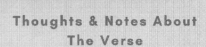

Daily Verse

DATE:_____

Bible Verse:

Thoughts & Notes About The Verse

Prayer Requests:

WEEKLY VERSE SUMMARY

M

T

W

TH

FRI

SAT

SUN

Church Notes

VERSES MENTIONED DURING CHURCH

☐ _____ ☐ _____
☐ _____ ☐ _____
☐ _____ ☐ _____
☐ _____ ☐ _____

OVERALL MESSAGE FROM SERMON

MY NOTES

PRAYER REQUESTS

My Notes

Daily Verse

DATE:_____

Bible Verse:

Thoughts & Notes About The Verse

Prayer Requests:

Daily Verse

DATE:_____

Bible Verse:

Thoughts & Notes About The Verse

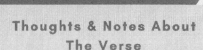

Prayer Requests:

Daily Verse

DATE: _____

Bible Verse:

**Thoughts & Notes About
The Verse**

Prayer Requests:

Daily Verse

DATE:_____

Bible Verse:

**Thoughts & Notes About
The Verse**

Prayer Requests:

Daily Verse

DATE:_____

Bible Verse:

**Thoughts & Notes About
The Verse**

Prayer Requests:

Daily Verse

DATE:_____

Bible Verse:

Thoughts & Notes About The Verse

Prayer Requests:

WEEKLY VERSE SUMMARY

M

T

W

TH

FRI

SAT

SUN

Church Notes

VERSES MENTIONED DURING CHURCH

- [ ] _____
- [ ] _____
- [ ] _____
- [ ] _____
- [ ] _____
- [ ] _____
- [ ] _____

OVERALL MESSAGE FROM SERMON

MY NOTES

PRAYER REQUESTS

My Notes

Thank you so much for buying this journal and adding it to your weekly prayer and bible study routine!

I really hope you found this journal helpful for organizing your prayers and bible verses.

Don't forget to check out my other journals!
(All available on Amazon & soon to local Indie book stores in Kalamazoo & Portage MI.)

Your reviews are always appreciated!

I love getting emails from my readers-drop me a line at:
jenniferlairdauthor@gmail.com

Kids Journals
Every Day Unicorn Journal
Every Day Mermaid Journal
Every Day Kitten Journal

Women's Journals
Coffee is Brewtiful
You've Got This
Every Day Journal

Prayer Journals
Prayer Journal

Coming Soon!
Gratitude Journal for Kids

Made in the USA
Columbia, SC
02 February 2025

53191719R00057